W9-CFB-167

WELCOME TO THE U.S.A.

INDIANA

Written by Ann Heinrichs   Illustrated by Matt Kania
Content Adviser: Nancy Wolfe, Educational Consultant,
Indianapolis, Indiana

The Child's World

Published in the United States of America by The Child's World®
PO Box 326 • Chanhassen, MN 55317-0326
800-599-READ • www.childsworld.com

Photo Credits
Cover: Indiana Office of Tourism Development; frontispiece: Indiana Office of Tourism Development.

Interior: Patrick Bennett/Corbis: 21, 29; Angela Bruntlett/Tippecanoe County Historical Association: 13; Corbis: 21 (Patrick Bennett), 25, 26 (Michael Kim), 34 (Layne Kennedy); Frank Doughman/Spirit of Vincennes, Inc.: 14; Indiana Office of Tourism Development: 6, 9, 17, 18, 22; Mike Linderman/Angel Mounds State Historic Site: 10; Kokomo Opalescent Glass: 30; Science Central: 33.

Acknowledgments
The Child's World®: Mary Berendes, Publishing Director

Editorial Directions, Inc.: E. Russell Primm, Editorial Director; Katie Marsico, Associate Editor; Judith Shiffer, Assistant Editor; Matt Messbarger, Editorial Assistant; Susan Hindman, Copy Editor; Melissa McDaniel, Proofreader; Kevin Cunningham, Peter Garnham, Matt Messbarger, Olivia Nellums, Chris Simms, Molly Symmonds, Katherine Trickle, Carl Stephen Wender, Fact Checkers; Tim Griffin/IndexServ, Indexer; Cian Loughlin O'Day, Photo Researcher and Editor

The Design Lab: Kathleen Petelinsek, Design; Julia Goozen, Art Production

Copyright © 2006 by The Child's World®
All rights reserved. No part of this book may be reproduced or utilized in any form or by any means without written permission from the publisher.

Library of Congress Cataloging-in-Publication Data
Heinrichs, Ann.
    Indiana / by Ann Heinrichs ; cartography and illustrations by Matt Kania.
      p. cm. — (Welcome to the U.S.A.)
    Includes index.
    ISBN 1-59296-472-9 (library bound : alk. paper) 1. Indiana—Juvenile literature.
I. Kania, Matt, ill. II. Title.
    F526.3.H45 2006
    977.2—dc22   2005010388

Ann Heinrichs is the author of more than 100 books for children and young adults. She has also enjoyed successful careers as a children's book editor and an advertising copywriter. Ann grew up in Fort Smith, Arkansas, and lives in Chicago, Illinois.

About the Author Ann Heinrichs

Matt Kania loves maps and, as a kid, dreamed of making them. In school he studied geography and cartography, and today he makes maps for a living. Matt's favorite thing about drawing maps is learning about the places they represent. Many of the maps he has created can be found in books, magazines, videos, Web sites, and public places.

About the Map Illustrator Matt Kania

On the cover: Visit Indianapolis to see the city lights sparkle!
On page one: Do you like boats? Watch them sail by at the Michigan City shore!

OUR INDIANA TRIP

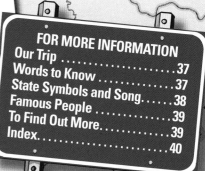

4

WELCOME TO
INDIANA

Are you up for a trip through Indiana? You'll find it's a great place to explore!

You'll ride a **canal** boat and watch car races. You'll hang out with **pioneers.** You'll watch people making glass. You'll make big bubbles and play with your shadow. You'll climb sand dunes much taller than a house. You'll see wild turkeys and deer. And you'll make candles and milk a cow!

Is this your kind of fun? Then settle in and buckle up. We're on our way!

As you travel through Indiana, watch for all the interesting facts along the way.

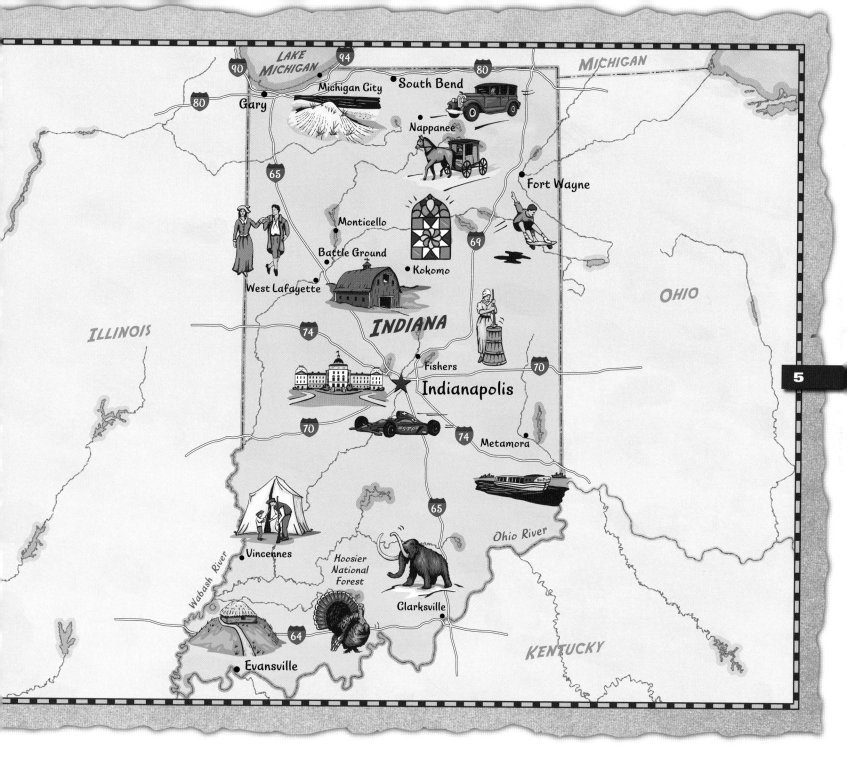

LAKE MICHIGAN

MICHIGAN

Gary

Michigan City

South Bend

Nappanee

Fort Wayne

Monticello

Battle Ground

West Lafayette

Kokomo

INDIANA

ILLINOIS

OHIO

Fishers

Indianapolis

Metamora

Vincennes

Hoosier National Forest

Clarksville

Ohio River

Wabash River

Evansville

KENTUCKY

Explore the trails at Dunes State Park.
Just don't forget the sunscreen!

Central and northern Indiana are part of the nation's Corn Belt. This part of the Midwest has rich, dark soil for growing corn and other crops.

6

Exploring the Indiana Dunes

Hike along miles of beaches. Explore the marshy wetlands. Roam through a forest. Or climb a sand dune.

You're exploring Indiana Dunes National Lakeshore! It runs along the Lake Michigan shore. It stretches from Gary to Michigan City.

Northwest Indiana faces Lake Michigan. This lake is one of the five Great Lakes. Fertile plains cover central Indiana. Its rich soil makes great farmland.

Southern Indiana is hilly. In some places, streams flow underground. The streams have created many spooky caves. The Ohio River creates Indiana's southern border. The Wabash River flows into it. The Wabash forms part of Indiana's western border.

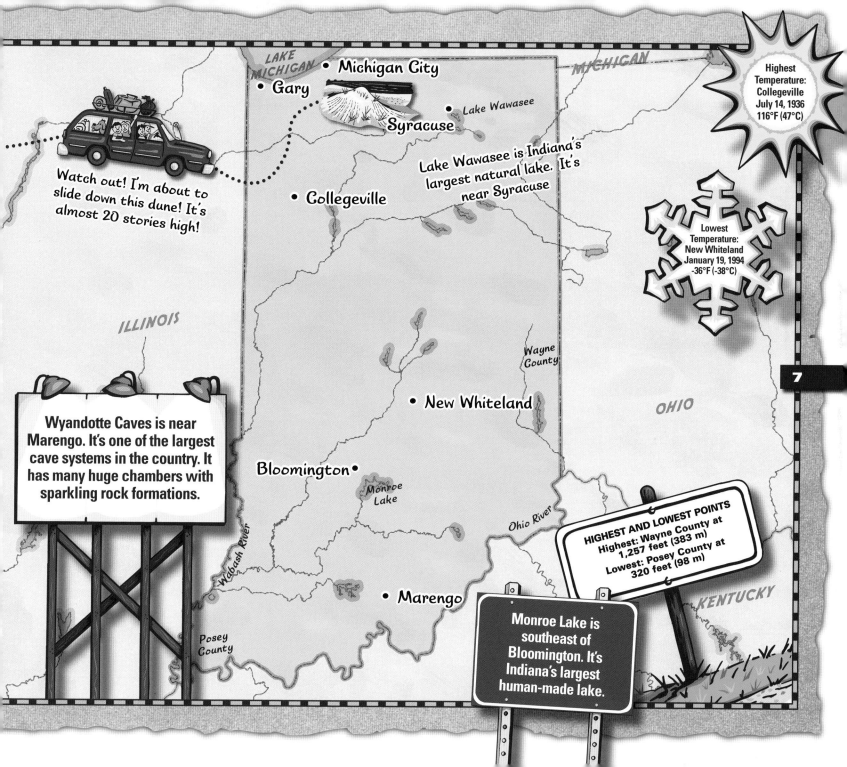

LAKE MICHIGAN

• Michigan City

• Gary

Syracuse

• Lake Wawasee

MICHIGAN

Watch out! I'm about to slide down this dune! It's almost 20 stories high!

• Collegeville

Lake Wawasee is Indiana's largest natural lake. It's near Syracuse

Highest Temperature: Collegeville July 14, 1936 116°F (47°C)

Lowest Temperature: New Whiteland January 19, 1994 -36°F (-38°C)

ILLINOIS

Wayne County

• New Whiteland

OHIO

Wyandotte Caves is near Marengo. It's one of the largest cave systems in the country. It has many huge chambers with sparkling rock formations.

Bloomington•

Monroe Lake

Ohio River

Wabash River

HIGHEST AND LOWEST POINTS
Highest: Wayne County at 1,257 feet (383 m)
Lowest: Posey County at 320 feet (98 m)

Posey County

• Marengo

Monroe Lake is southeast of Bloomington. It's Indiana's largest human-made lake.

KENTUCKY

Turkey quiz time! What are male turkeys called? They're called gobblers or toms!

STATE FLOWER
PEONY

STATE TREE
TULIP TREE
(YELLOW POPLAR0

STATE BIRD
CARDINAL

MICHIGAN

ILLINOIS

OHIO

• Battle Ground

• Nashville

• Seymour

• Madison

Hoosier
National
Forest

KENTUCKY

• Tell City

Muscatatuck National Wildlife Refuge is near Seymour. River otters were introduced there in 1995. The refuge is also known for its many waterbirds.

Wolf Park in Battle Ground is home to a pack of wolves. You'll hear the wolves howl at night. Foxes, bison, and coyotes live there, too.

The National Park Service has 3 sites in Indiana.

Wildlife in Hoosier National Forest

Female turkeys are called hens. Their babies are called poults.

Sneak softly through Hoosier National Forest. A shy deer may peek out at you. Foxes, woodchucks, and squirrels scurry here and there. You might come upon a female wild turkey. Her babies waddle along behind her.

Near a stream, you may see beavers. They build their lodges with sticks and grass. Herons and egrets live near the water, too. Hawks and eagles soar high overhead.

Hoosier National Forest covers much of southern Indiana. It's a great place for watching wildlife. The forest is made of four big sections. Its northern end is near Nashville. Its southern end is near Tell City.

This wolf calls an Indiana forest home.

Big Oaks National Wildlife Refuge is near Madison. Many kinds of birds, bats, butterflies, and mammals live there.

Several thousand people lived at Angel Mounds.

Want to take a trip back in time? Just visit Angel Mounds.

Angel Mounds in Evansville

Stroll through the village houses. Life-size figures are all around you. Some are hunting or making meals. Others are playing games. You're visiting Angel Mounds!

Native Americans called Mound Builders once lived here. They grew corn, beans, squash, and pumpkins. They hunted in the forests. There they found deer, squirrels, and wild turkeys.

You'll see the huge earthen mounds they created. Chiefs and nobles built homes on the mounds. Some mounds had temples on top. Priests held religious ceremonies there. People from miles around traveled to Angel Mounds. They came to trade goods and attend ceremonies.

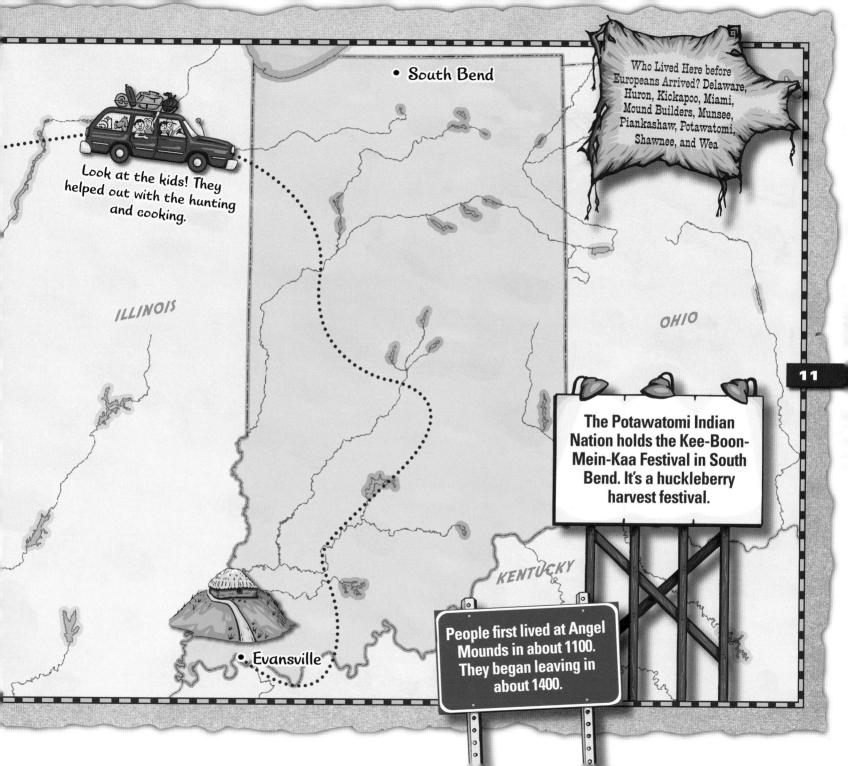

Look at the kids! They helped out with the hunting and cooking.

South Bend

ILLINOIS

OHIO

Who Lived Here before Europeans Arrived? Delaware, Huron, Kickapoo, Miami, Mound Builders, Munsee, Piankashaw, Potawatomi, Shawnee, and Wea

The Potawatomi Indian Nation holds the Kee-Boon-Mein-Kaa Festival in South Bend. It's a huckleberry harvest festival.

KENTUCKY

People first lived at Angel Mounds in about 1100. They began leaving in about 1400.

Evansville

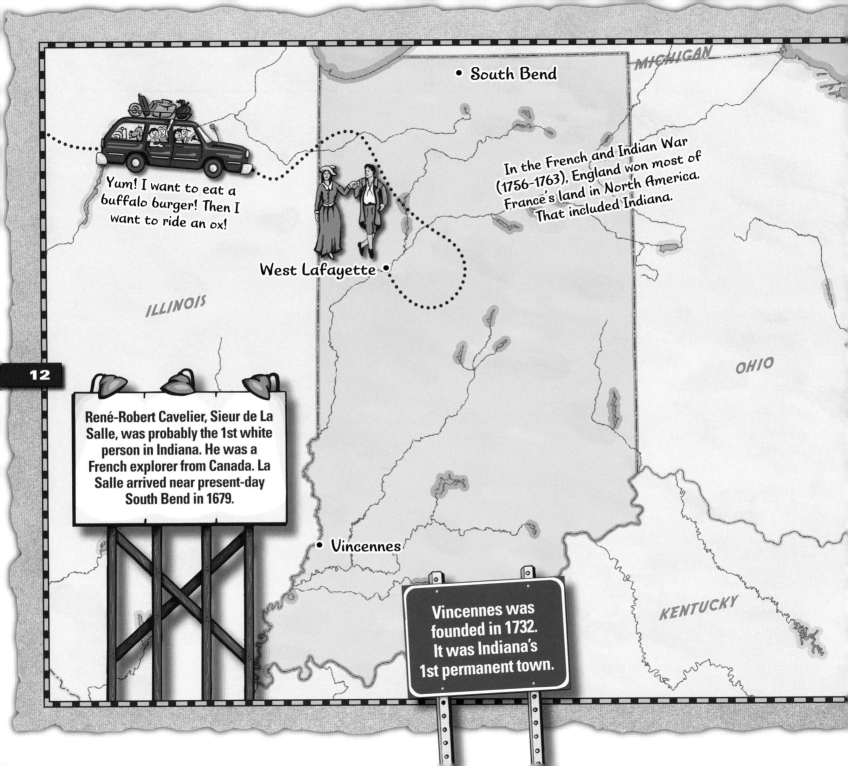

MICHIGAN

• South Bend

Yum! I want to eat a
buffalo burger! Then I
want to ride an ox!

In the French and Indian War
(1756–1763), England won most of
France's land in North America.
That included Indiana.

West Lafayette •

ILLINOIS

OHIO

René-Robert Cavelier, Sieur de La
Salle, was probably the 1st white
person in Indiana. He was a
French explorer from Canada. La
Salle arrived near present-day
South Bend in 1679.

• Vincennes

KENTUCKY

Vincennes was
founded in 1732.
It was Indiana's
1st permanent town.

The Feast of the Hunters' Moon

Make a hand-dipped candle. String some Indian beads. Or try on some 1700s clothes. It's the Feast of the Hunters' Moon! This festival recalls Indiana's olden days. It takes place at Fort Ouiatenon in West Lafayette.

Fur traders were early explorers in Indiana. They were Frenchmen from Canada, to the north. They traded goods with the Indians for furs. Fort Ouiatenon was built in 1717. It was a fur-trading post.

Every fall, the French and Indians gathered there. They celebrated the Feast of the Hunters' Moon. It was a chance to make friendships stronger. People shared their stories, food, and games.

What games did kids play in the 1700s? Find out at the Feast of the Hunters' Moon.

14

The Spirit of Vincennes Rendezvous

Ready, aim, fire! You're watching a historical reenactment in Vincennes.

The Spirit of Vincennes Rendezvous takes place at George Rogers Clark National Historical Park in Vincennes.

Pow! Cannons are booming. **Muskets** are firing. It's the Spirit of Vincennes **Rendezvous**!

This event celebrates a great victory in 1779. The Revolutionary War (1775–1783) was going on. **Colonists** were fighting for freedom from British rule.

British troops captured Fort Sackville at Vincennes. George Rogers Clark hoped to win it back. His soldiers snuck into Vincennes and surprised the British. At last, they won the fort!

Colonial times come to life at the rendezvous. People dress like the settlers did. They act out battles and demonstrate colonial crafts. Kids ride ponies and play colonial games. Drop by and enjoy the fun!

Indiana was the 19th state to enter the Union. It joined on December 11, 1816.

Hey, look! We can try trundling the hoop, stilt walking, and ninepins! Kids played these games in the 1700s.

ILLINOIS

OHIO

The British surrendered Fort Sackville on February 25, 1779.

• Vincennes

The United States set up the Northwest Territory in 1787. It included what is now Indiana, as well as several other states.

KENTUCKY

The 1st public **subscription** library in Indiana opened in Vincennes in 1807.

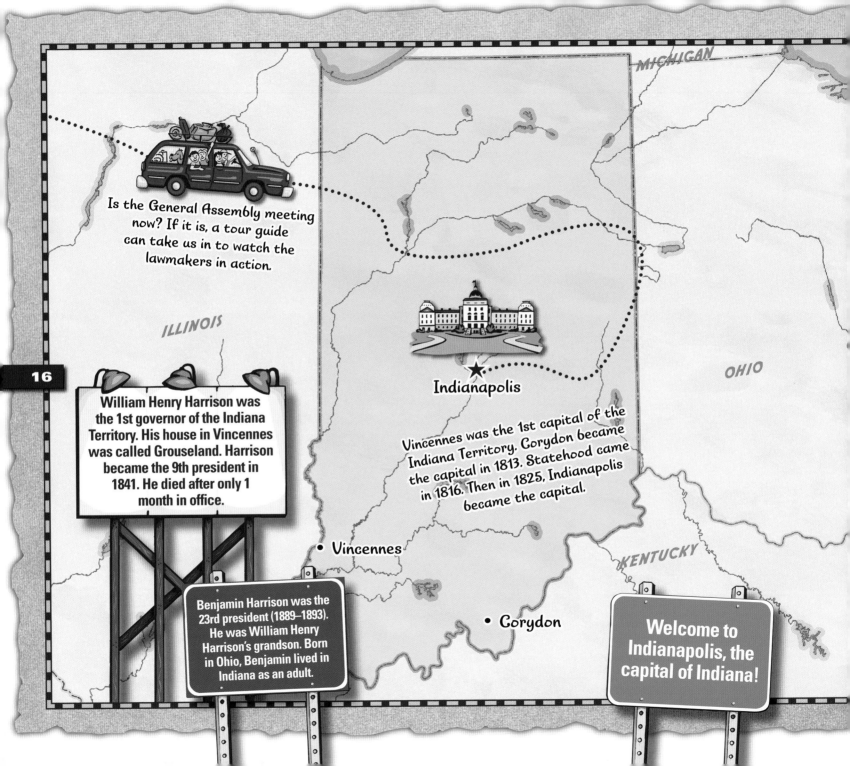

Is the General Assembly meeting now? If it is, a tour guide can take us in to watch the lawmakers in action.

MICHIGAN

ILLINOIS

OHIO

Indianapolis

Vincennes was the 1st capital of the Indiana Territory. Corydon became the capital in 1813. Statehood came in 1816. Then in 1825, Indianapolis became the capital.

16

William Henry Harrison was the 1st governor of the Indiana Territory. His house in Vincennes was called Grouseland. Harrison became the 9th president in 1841. He died after only 1 month in office.

• Vincennes

Benjamin Harrison was the 23rd president (1889–1893). He was William Henry Harrison's grandson. Born in Ohio, Benjamin lived in Indiana as an adult.

• Corydon

KENTUCKY

Welcome to Indianapolis, the capital of Indiana!

The State Capitol in Indianapolis

The state capitol is a grand building. And no wonder. It's the center of state government! Many important decisions are made here. These decisions affect everyone in the state.

Indiana has three branches of government. All three branches meet in the capitol. One branch passes state laws. Its members belong to the General Assembly. Another branch makes sure the laws are carried out. The governor heads this branch. Judges make up the third branch. They decide whether laws have been broken.

The dome atop Indiana's capitol shines brightly at night.

Indiana's state motto is "The Crossroads of America."

What year is it? Experience pioneer life at Conner Prairie.

Conner Prairie holds classes that teach kids many pioneer crafts.

Pioneer Life at Conner Prairie

How did Indiana's pioneers live? Step back in time and see for yourself. Just visit Conner Prairie in Fishers!

You'll grind corn in an Indian camp. You'll take a class in the one-room schoolhouse. You'll milk a cow and churn butter. You'll see that pioneers really kept busy!

Many pioneers moved into Indiana. They had heard how rich the soil was. They cleared land and planted crops. Indians and settlers often clashed, though.

The Indians didn't want to lose their homeland, but they did. Some of it was taken after they lost battles. Other land was purchased by the U.S. government.

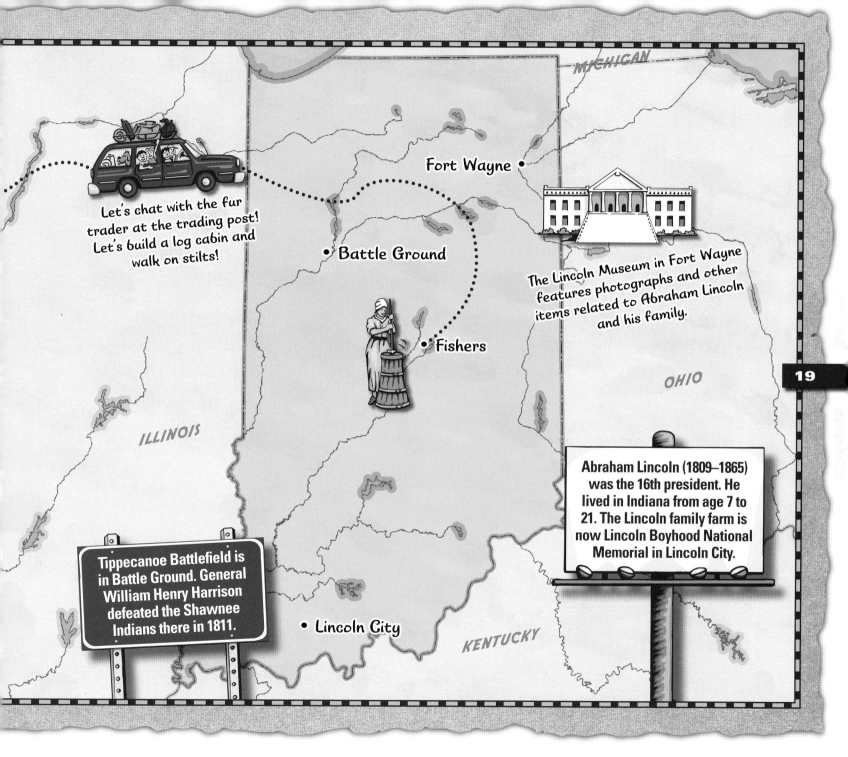

Let's chat with the fur trader at the trading post! Let's build a log cabin and walk on stilts!

MICHIGAN

Fort Wayne

Battle Ground

Fishers

The Lincoln Museum in Fort Wayne features photographs and other items related to Abraham Lincoln and his family.

ILLINOIS

OHIO

Abraham Lincoln (1809–1865) was the 16th president. He lived in Indiana from age 7 to 21. The Lincoln family farm is now Lincoln Boyhood National Memorial in Lincoln City.

Tippecanoe Battlefield is in Battle Ground. General William Henry Harrison defeated the Shawnee Indians there in 1811.

Lincoln City

KENTUCKY

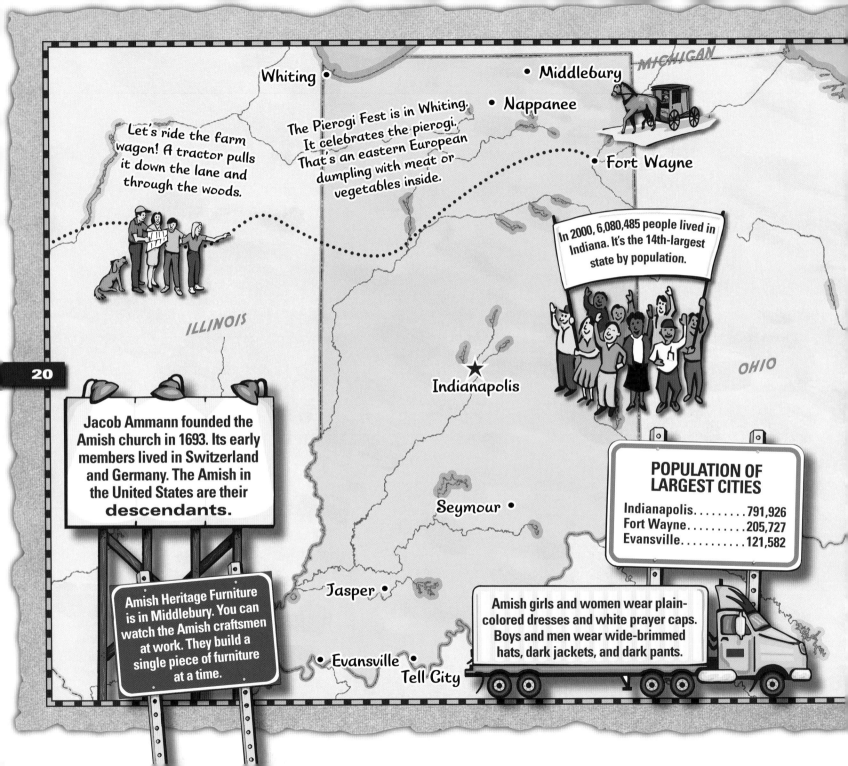

Whiting •

• Middlebury

MICHIGAN

• Nappanee

Let's ride the farm wagon! A tractor pulls it down the lane and through the woods.

The Pierogi Fest is in Whiting. It celebrates the pierogi. That's an eastern European dumpling with meat or vegetables inside.

• Fort Wayne

In 2000, 6,080,485 people lived in Indiana. It's the 14th-largest state by population.

ILLINOIS

★
Indianapolis

OHIO

Jacob Ammann founded the Amish church in 1693. Its early members lived in Switzerland and Germany. The Amish in the United States are their **descendants.**

Seymour •

POPULATION OF LARGEST CITIES

Indianapolis.........791,926
Fort Wayne..........205,727
Evansville...........121,582

Amish Heritage Furniture is in Middlebury. You can watch the Amish craftsmen at work. They build a single piece of furniture at a time.

Jasper •

Amish girls and women wear plain-colored dresses and white prayer caps. Boys and men wear wide-brimmed hats, dark jackets, and dark pants.

• Evansville •

Tell City

Amish Acres in Nappanee

Ride around on a horse-drawn buggy. You may see people weaving or making brooms. Someone in the barn might be shoeing horses.

You're visiting Amish Acres! There you learn how Indiana's Amish people live.

The Amish are a religious group. They dress plainly and lead simple farming lives. They ride in horse-drawn buggies instead of cars. They don't use electricity and other modern devices.

The Amish first came to Indiana in 1839. They are known for making sturdy furniture by hand. Their handmade quilts are beautiful. Amish cooking and baked goods are delicious, too!

Watch craftsmen work at Amish Acres. Who knew making a broom could be so hard?

Indiana's German festivals include Schweitzerfest in Tell City, Strassenfest in Jasper, and Oktoberfest in Seymour.

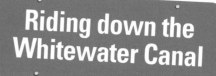

Riding down the Whitewater Canal

Hop aboard the *Ben Franklin III*. You board this canal boat in Metamora. There's a sturdy horse walking along the shore. He's pulling your boat!

Then check out the mill. You'll see it grind corn into cornmeal. The canal waters turn its mill wheel around. You're exploring the Whitewater Canal!

People began digging this canal in the 1830s. Canals were great for transportation. Farmers used them to ship goods. That was much faster than land travel. People traveled on canal boats, too. That was easier than riding through the wilderness!

Giddyup! A horse pulls a boat along the Whitewater Canal.

The Whitewater Canal ran between Hagerstown and Lawrenceburg. From Lawrenceburg, a spur canal continued into Ohio.

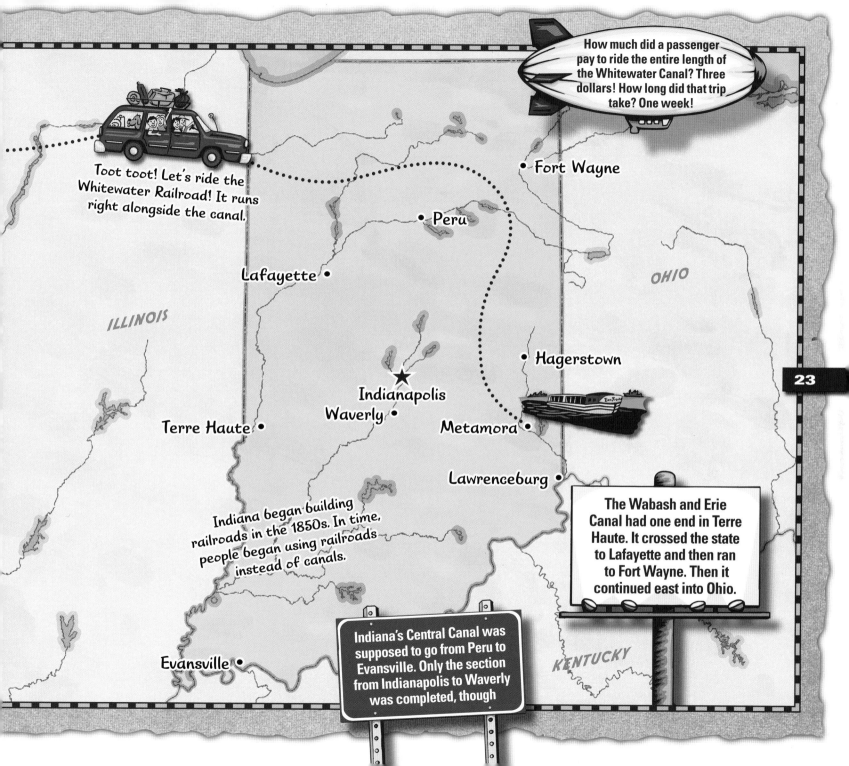

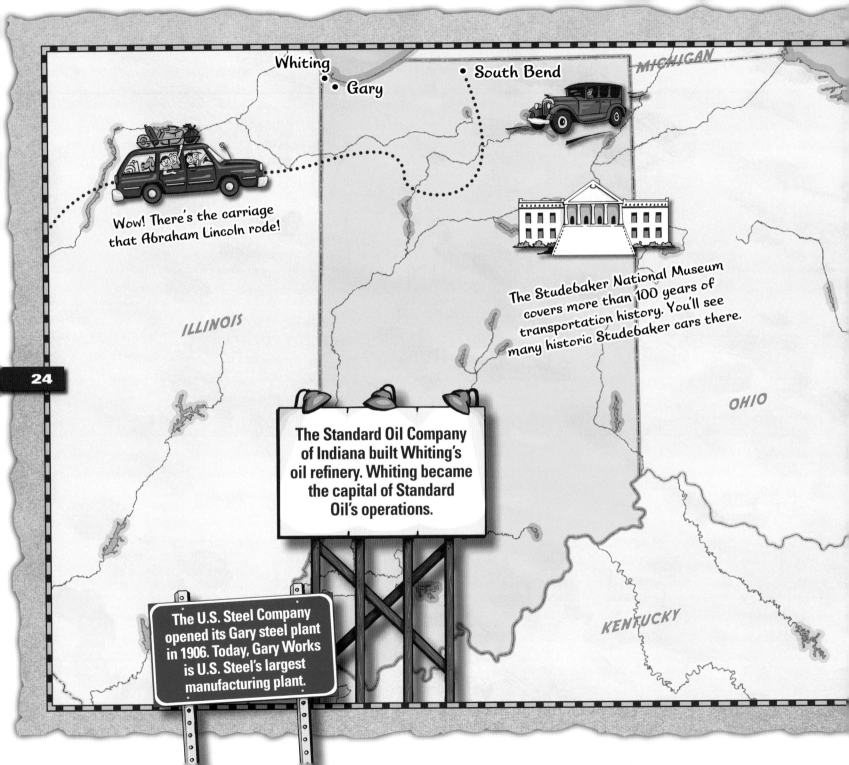

Whiting

Gary

South Bend

MICHIGAN

Wow! There's the carriage that Abraham Lincoln rode!

ILLINOIS

OHIO

The Studebaker National Museum covers more than 100 years of transportation history. You'll see many historic Studebaker cars there.

The Standard Oil Company of Indiana built Whiting's oil refinery. Whiting became the capital of Standard Oil's operations.

KENTUCKY

The U.S. Steel Company opened its Gary steel plant in 1906. Today, Gary Works is U.S. Steel's largest manufacturing plant.

See an old covered wagon. Walk on, and look at some antique cars. You'll even see some presidents' coaches. You're touring the Studebaker National Museum!

Clement and Henry Studebaker were brothers. They opened a horse-drawn wagon shop in 1852. But they saw what the future held—cars! They built an electric car in 1902. Next, they developed cars that ran on gasoline. The Studebaker company built cars until 1966.

Many other **industries** helped Indiana grow. An oil-**refining** plant opened in Whiting in 1889. It produced gasoline for cars. Steel mills opened in Gary, too.

They don't make 'em like this anymore! Check out some cool cars in South Bend!

25

Who will make it to the finish line first?
Don't miss the Indianapolis 500!

The Indianapolis 500

Vroom! And they're off! The colorful cars zoom around the track. Some go more than 200 miles (300 kilometers) an hour. It's the Indianapolis 500!

This is a world-famous car race. Racing fans come from all over to watch. It takes place in Speedway, near Indianapolis.

Indiana is also known for its basketball games. High school games are especially popular. State tournament time in March is wild. It's called Hoosier Hysteria!

For quieter fun, people enjoy the outdoors. They hike along the dunes or through forests.

Indianapolis 500 racers go around the track 200 times. Their total distance is 500 miles (805 km).

South Bend

The 1st Indianapolis 500 car race took place in 1911.

Guess what the winner does after the race? Drinks milk in Victory Lane! The winner did that in 1936. Now all winners do it!

ILLINOIS

Marion •

The Indiana Basketball Hall of Fame is in New Castle.

• New Castle

OHIO

★ Indianapolis

MICHIGAN

Cartoonist Jim Davis created the comic strip *Garfield*. Davis was born on a cow farm in Marion.

The College Football Hall of Fame is in South Bend.

KENTUCKY

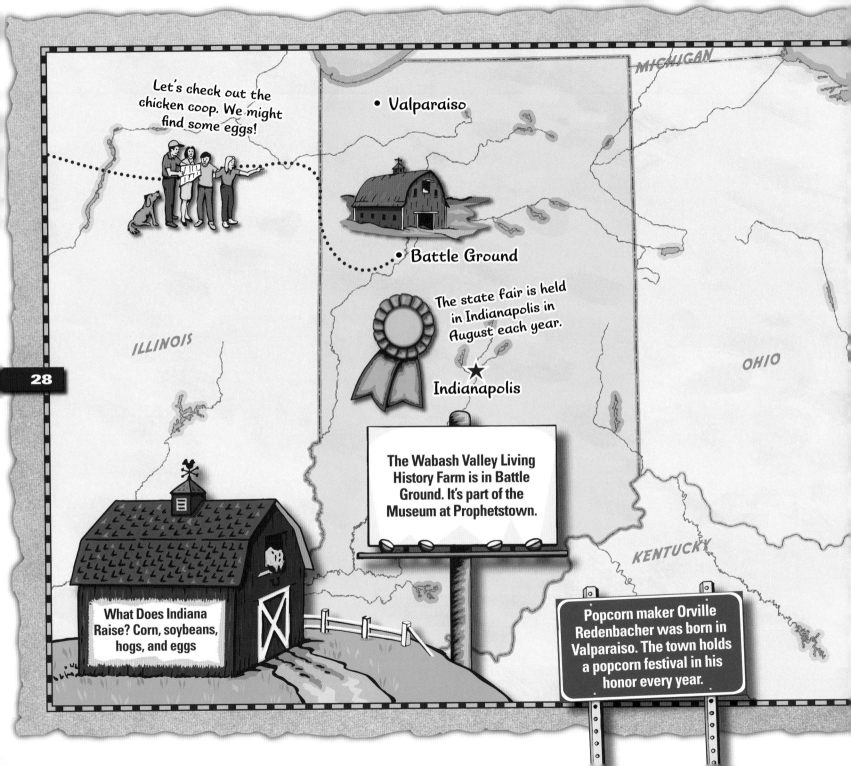

Wabash Valley Living History Farm

What goes on inside the barn? Horses munch on their hay. A farmer milks a cow. And cats stand by, hoping for some milk!

Now look around the farmyard. Workers load hay onto wagons with pitchforks. You might see new baby horses or sheep. You can pet them if they don't run away!

You're exploring the Wabash Valley Living History Farm. It's just like a farm in the 1920s. Farming has always been important in Indiana. Corn and soybeans are the top crops today. Some of that corn ends up as popcorn!

Indiana's most valuable farm animals are hogs.

Whoa! Indiana farmers are still working hard today.

29

Making Glass in Kokomo

Have you ever seen stained-glass windows? Want to learn how they're made? Just tour Kokomo Opalescent Glass.

You'll see fiery furnaces melting the glass. Workers pick up melted glass with big **ladles.** They pour different colors of glass together. Rollers roll the glass into sheets. It's hard work. But the results are beautiful!

Glass is only one of Indiana's factory goods. Transportation equipment is the leading factory product. That includes cars, recreational vehicles, and airplane parts. Steel is a major product, too. Most steel plants are in cities along Lake Michigan. Their smokestacks rise high into the sky.

Ever wonder how glass is made? You'll find out if you visit Kokomo.

Gary's nickname is Steel City because of its big U.S. Steel plant.

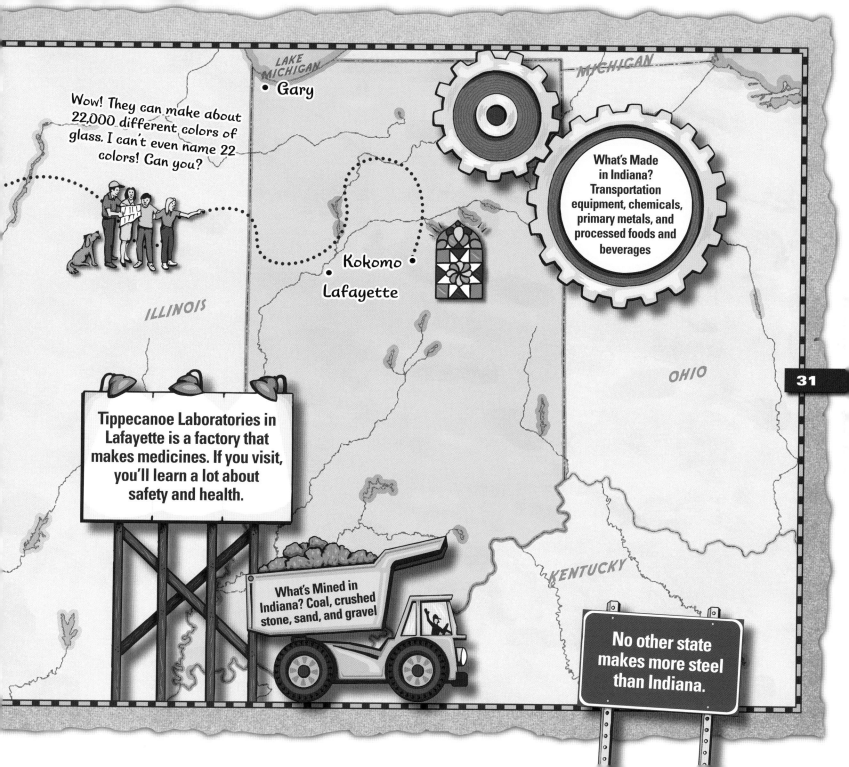

Wow! They can make about 22,000 different colors of glass. I can't even name 22 colors! Can you?

LAKE MICHIGAN

• Gary

MICHIGAN

ILLINOIS

Kokomo •
Lafayette

What's Made in Indiana? Transportation equipment, chemicals, primary metals, and processed foods and beverages

OHIO

Tippecanoe Laboratories in Lafayette is a factory that makes medicines. If you visit, you'll learn a lot about safety and health.

What's Mined in Indiana? Coal, crushed stone, sand, and gravel

KENTUCKY

No other state makes more steel than Indiana.

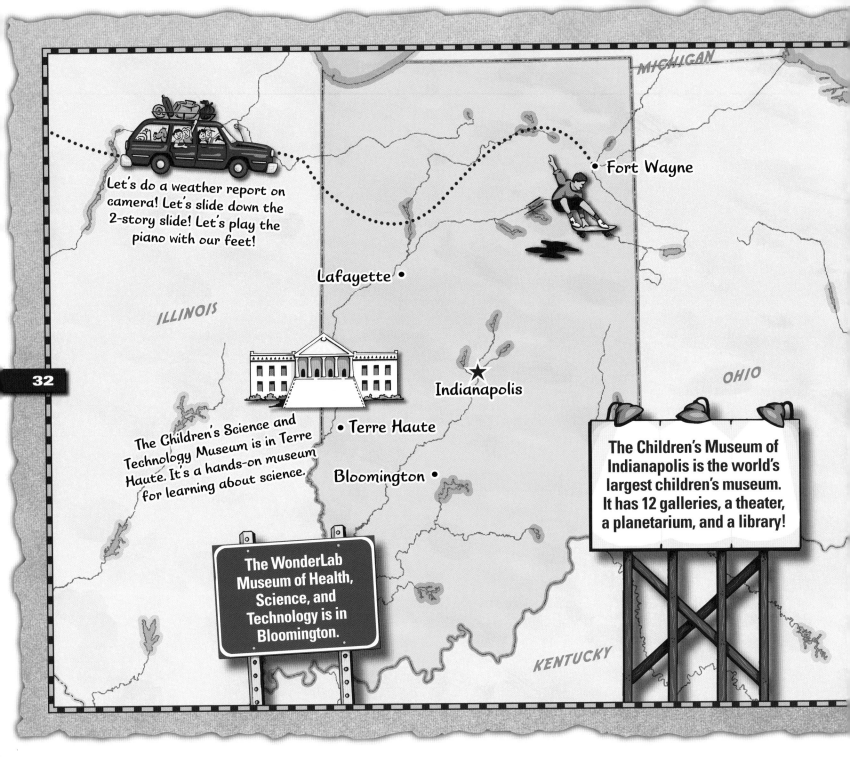

MICHIGAN

• Fort Wayne

Let's do a weather report on camera! Let's slide down the 2-story slide! Let's play the piano with our feet!

Lafayette •

ILLINOIS

OHIO

The Children's Science and Technology Museum is in Terre Haute. It's a hands-on museum for learning about science.

Indianapolis

Terre Haute

Bloomington •

The Children's Museum of Indianapolis is the world's largest children's museum. It has 12 galleries, a theater, a planetarium, and a library!

The WonderLab Museum of Health, Science, and Technology is in Bloomington.

KENTUCKY

Fort Wayne's Science Central

The Imagination Station is a hands-on science museum in Lafayette.

Play with your own shadow. Make a bubble as big as you. See how much water is inside you. And go cycling with a skeleton!

Do all this and more at Science Central. It's an amazing science museum. Kids love to explore and learn new things there. They discover the wonders of science!

Scientific discoveries brought Indiana into the modern world. Hundreds of Indiana companies make computer-related equipment. Some equipment makes factories run. Other equipment creates faster ways to communicate. And some equipment has medical uses. Inventors of all these devices began as curious kids!

Would you make a good scientist? Be sure to stop by Science Central!

Indiana has more than 500 companies in **high-tech** industries.

A giant woolly **mammoth** skeleton greets you. A huge fish seems to swim overhead. You're visiting the Falls of the Ohio State Park. And you've just walked into the visitors' center.

Thousands of **fossils** were discovered in this area. Some are more than 350 million years old!

This site is in Clarksville. It's right by the Ohio River. An ancient sea once covered this area. Land and sea creatures left their remains behind.

You'll see all kinds of fossils here. One fish skull is almost as tall as you. Good thing you weren't going swimming millions of years ago!

Want to see some huge fossils? Head to the Falls of the Ohio State Park.

Clarksville is just across the Ohio River from Louisville, Kentucky.

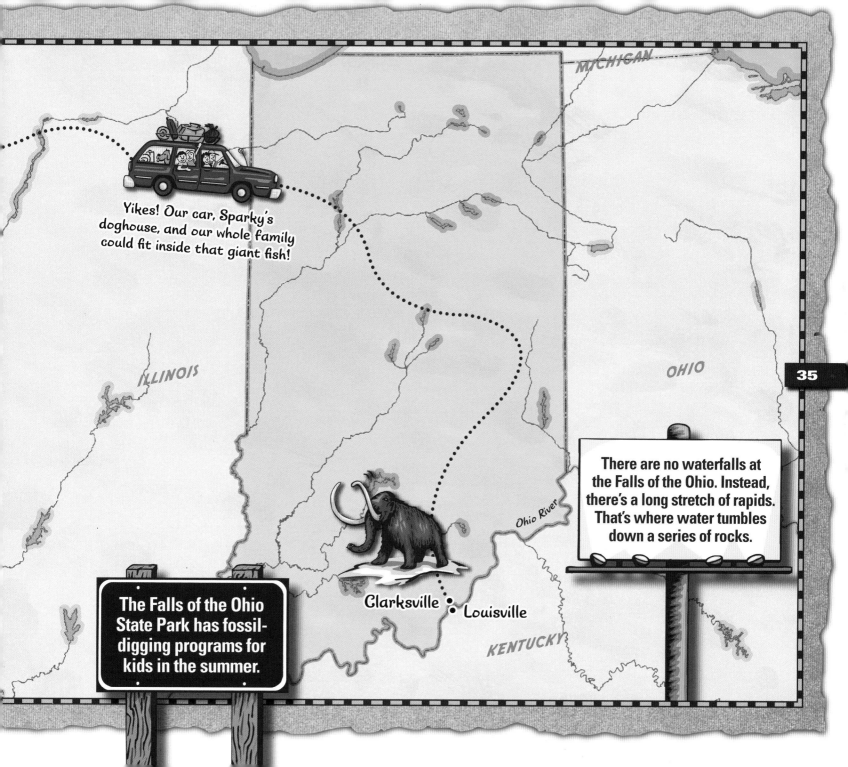

Yikes! Our car, Sparky's doghouse, and our whole family could fit inside that giant fish!

The Falls of the Ohio State Park has fossil-digging programs for kids in the summer.

There are no waterfalls at the Falls of the Ohio. Instead, there's a long stretch of rapids. That's where water tumbles down a series of rocks.

MICHIGAN

ILLINOIS

OHIO

Ohio River

Clarksville • Louisville

KENTUCKY

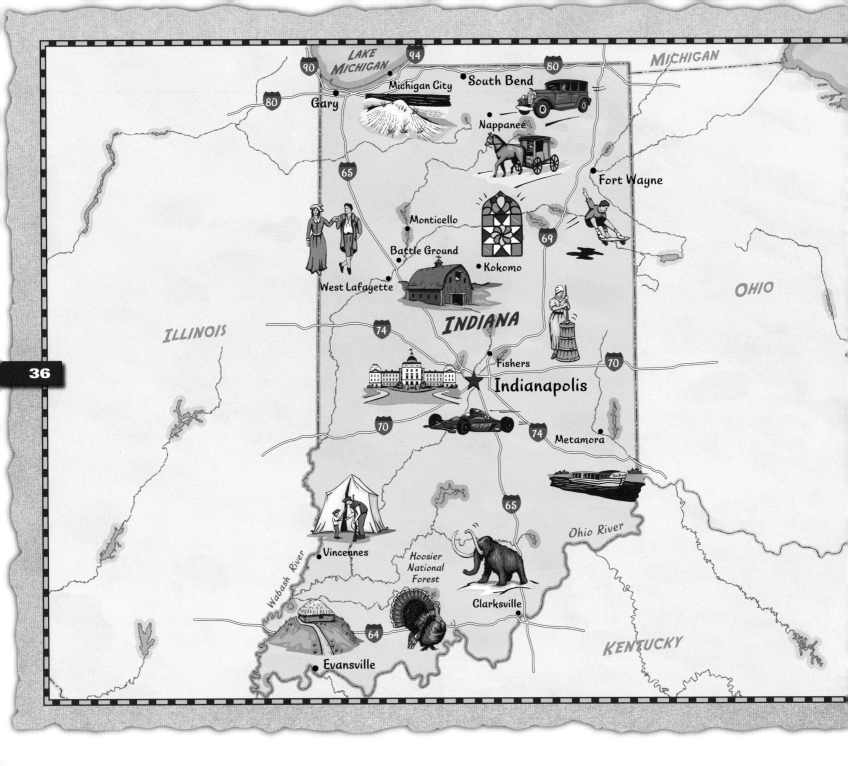

LAKE MICHIGAN

94

90

80

MICHIGAN

Michigan City

South Bend

Gary

Nappanee

Fort Wayne

65

Monticello

69

Battle Ground

West Lafayette

Kokomo

INDIANA

OHIO

74

Fishers

70

Indianapolis

ILLINOIS

70

74

Metamora

65

Ohio River

Vincennes

Hoosier
National
Forest

Wabash River

Clarksville

64

KENTUCKY

Evansville

OUR TRIP

We visited many amazing places on our trip! We also met a lot of interesting people along the way. Look at the map on your left. Use your finger to trace all the places we have been.

What are female turkeys called? See page 9 for the answer.

What are some games kids played in the 1700s? Page 15 has the answer.

Where did Abraham Lincoln live in Indiana? See page 19 for the answer.

How much did it cost to ride the Whitewater Canal? Look on page 23 for the answer.

What is U.S. Steel's largest manufacturing plant? Page 24 has the answer.

When was the 1st Indianapolis 500 car race? Turn to page 27 for the answer.

What is Indiana's most valuable farm animal? Look on page 29 for the answer.

What is Gary's nickname? Turn to page 30 for the answer.

That was a great trip! We have traveled all over Indiana.

There are a few places that we didn't have time for, though. Next time, we plan to visit Indiana Beach Amusement Park in Monticello. It has roller coasters, rides, a lake, and a sand beach. There is even a giant water park!

More Places to Visit in Indiana

WORDS TO KNOW

canal (kuh-NAL) a long waterway dug by humans

colonists (KOL-uh-nihsts) people who settle in a land with ties to a mother country

descendants (di-SEND-uhnts) a person's children, grandchildren, great-grandchildren, and so on

fossils (FOSS-uhlz) prints or remains of plants and animals that lived long ago

high-tech (HI-TEHK) short for high-technology; using high-level electronics and computer devices

industries (IN-duh-streez) types of businesses

ladles (LAY-duhlz) big spoons that are like bowls with long handles

mammoth (MAMM-uth) a huge animal similar to an elephant that lived a long time ago

muskets (MUSS-kits) early types of rifles

pioneers (pie-uh-NEERZ) the 1st people to move into an unsettled area

refining (rih-FINE-ing) a process that removes extra material and cleans the remains

rendezvous (RON-day-voo) French word for a meeting

subscription (suhb-SKRIP-shuhn) a service that people regularly pay money for

Indiana covers 35,867 square miles (92,895 sq km). It's the 38th-largest state in size.

STATE SYMBOLS

State bird: Cardinal

State flower: Peony

State poem: "Indiana" by Arthur Franklin Mapes

State river: Wabash River

State stone: Limestone

State tree: Tulip tree (yellow poplar)

State flag

State seal

STATE SONG

"On the Banks of the Wabash, Far Away"

Words and music by Paul Dresser

'Round my Indiana homestead wave the cornfields,
In the distance loom the woodlands clear and cool.
Oftentimes my thoughts revert to scenes of childhood,
Where I first received my lessons, nature's school.
But one thing there is missing in the picture,
Without her face it seems so incomplete.
I long to see my mother in the doorway,
As she stood there years ago, her boy to greet.

Chorus:
Oh, the moonlight's fair tonight along the Wabash,
From the fields there comes the breath of newmown hay.
Through the sycamores the candle lights are gleaming,
On the banks of the Wabash, far away.

Many years have passed since I strolled by the river,
Arm in arm, with sweetheart Mary by my side,
It was there I tried to tell her that I loved her,
It was there I begged of her to be my bride.
Long years have passed since I strolled thro' the churchyard.
She's sleeping there, my angel, Mary dear,
I loved her, but she thought I didn't mean it,
Still I'd give my future were she only here.

FAMOUS PEOPLE

Bird, Larry (1956–), basketball player

Bridwell, Norman (1928–), children's author and illustrator

Coffin, Levi (1798–1877), abolitionist

Dean, James (1931–1955), actor

Dillinger, John (1903–1934), gangster

Dreiser, Theodore (1871–1945), author

Fraser, Brendan (1968–), actor

Grissom, Virgil (1926–1967), astronaut

Gordon, Jeff (1971–), NASCAR racer

Harrison, Benjamin (1833–1901), 23rd U.S. president

Letterman, David (1947–), comedian and television host

Mellencamp, John (1951–), singer and songwriter

Naylor, Phyllis Reynolds (1933–), children's author

Porter, Cole (1891–1964), songwriter

Pyle, Ernie (1900–1945), journalist

Riley, James Whitcomb (1849–1916), poet

Stewart, Tony (1971–), NASCAR racer

Tharp, Twyla (1941–), dancer and choreographer

Vonnegut, Kurt, Jr. (1922–), author

Walker, Madam C. J. (1867–1919), businesswoman and millionaire

White, Ryan (1971–1990), young AIDS victim and activist

Wright, Wilbur (1867–1912), inventor and pilot

TO FIND OUT MORE

At the Library

Buller, Jon, and Susan Schade. *The Wright Brothers Take Off.* New York: Grosset & Dunlap, 2003.

Francis, Sandra. *Benjamin Harrison: Our Twenty-Third President.* Chanhassen, Minn.: The Child's World, 2002.

McKissack, Patricia, and Fredrick McKissack. *Madam C. J. Walker: Self-Made Millionaire.* Berkeley Heights, N.J.: Enslow Publishers, 2001.

Reynolds, Cynthia Furlong, and Bruce Langton (illustrator). *H Is for Hoosier: An Indiana Alphabet.* Chelsea, Mich.: Sleeping Bear Press, 2001.

Riley, James Whitcomb, and Glenna Lang (illustrator). *When the Frost Is on the Punkin.* Boston: D. R. Godine, 1991.

On the Web

Visit our home page for lots of links about Indiana: *http://www.childsworld.com/links*

Note to Parents, Teachers, and Librarians: We routinely verify our Web links to make sure they are safe, active sites—so encourage your readers to check them out!

Places to Visit or Contact

Indiana Department of Commerce
Office of Tourism and Film Development
One North Capitol, Suite 700
Indianapolis, IN 46204
317/232-8860
For more information about traveling in Indiana

Indiana Historical Society
450 West Ohio Street
Indianapolis, IN 46202
317/232-1882
For more information about the history of Indiana

INDEX

Bye, Hoosier State.
We had a great time.
We'll come back soon!